ST. ANTHONY OF PADUA

1

Introduce children to the heartwarming life of Saint Anthony of Padua in this illustrated story and activity book. With soft, friendly artwork and storytelling, young readers follow St. Anthony from his early years through the miracles and lessons that made him beloved —discovering prayer, forgiveness, and service along the way

Interspersed with the story are engaging activity pages designed to deepen understanding while having fun:
- Color by Number and Coloring pages to bring Saint Anthony and his symbols to life
- Spot the Difference challenges that sharpen observation with scenes from his miracles
- Mazes and hidden object puzzles where kids help friends return lost items or deliver messages, reinforcing patience and problem-solving
- A Certificate of Completion to celebrate finishing the book and activities

Perfect for bedtime reading, faith formation, Sunday school, or quiet afternoons, this book blends gentle inspiration with hands-on play—helping kids reflect on virtue while they color, explore, and learn

Written, Designed and Published in the USA

DEDICATION

To Saint Anthony of Padua:
With gratitude for your constant intercession and the
many blessings received through Jesus and Mary. May your
example of faith and love inspire every child who turns
these pages

To our nephews Joel and his beloved brother Joshua:
Joel, your curiosity, daily check-ins, and eagerness to
share Saint Anthony with your little baby brother and
friends pushed us across the finish line. This book exists
because of your inspiration and enthusiasm.
May Saint Anthony guide you both

Aunty Diya and Uncle Joby

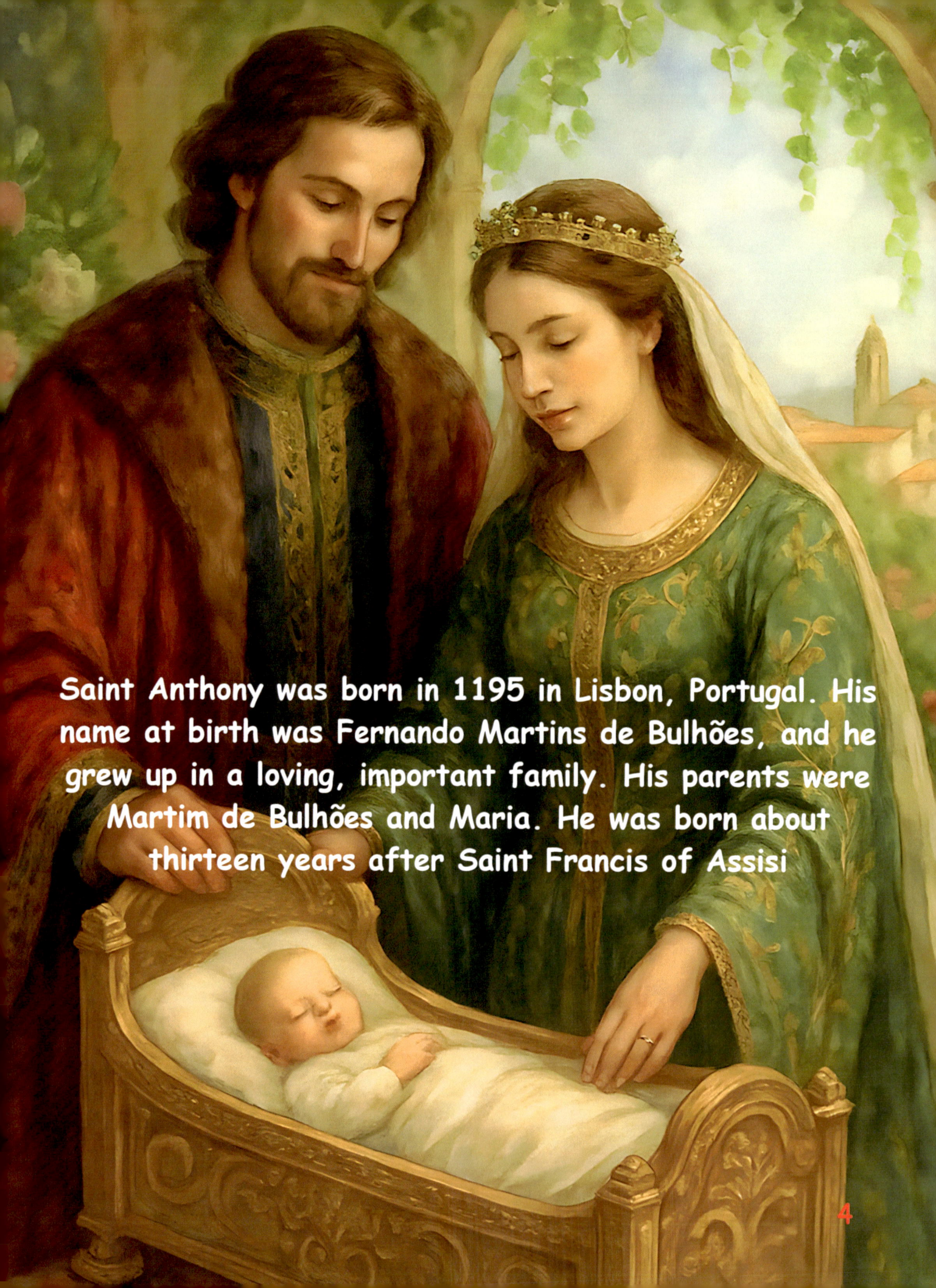

Saint Anthony was born in 1195 in Lisbon, Portugal. His name at birth was Fernando Martins de Bulhões, and he grew up in a loving, important family. His parents were Martim de Bulhões and Maria. He was born about thirteen years after Saint Francis of Assisi

He was the firstborn in the noble family, and his parents educated him well, hoping he would become a church leader or government official. But Ferdinand chose a different path—one of loving service to God

5

Once, while praying, a mean spirit tried to scare him—but Saint Anthony simply made the sign of the cross on the floor, and the spirit ran away!

6

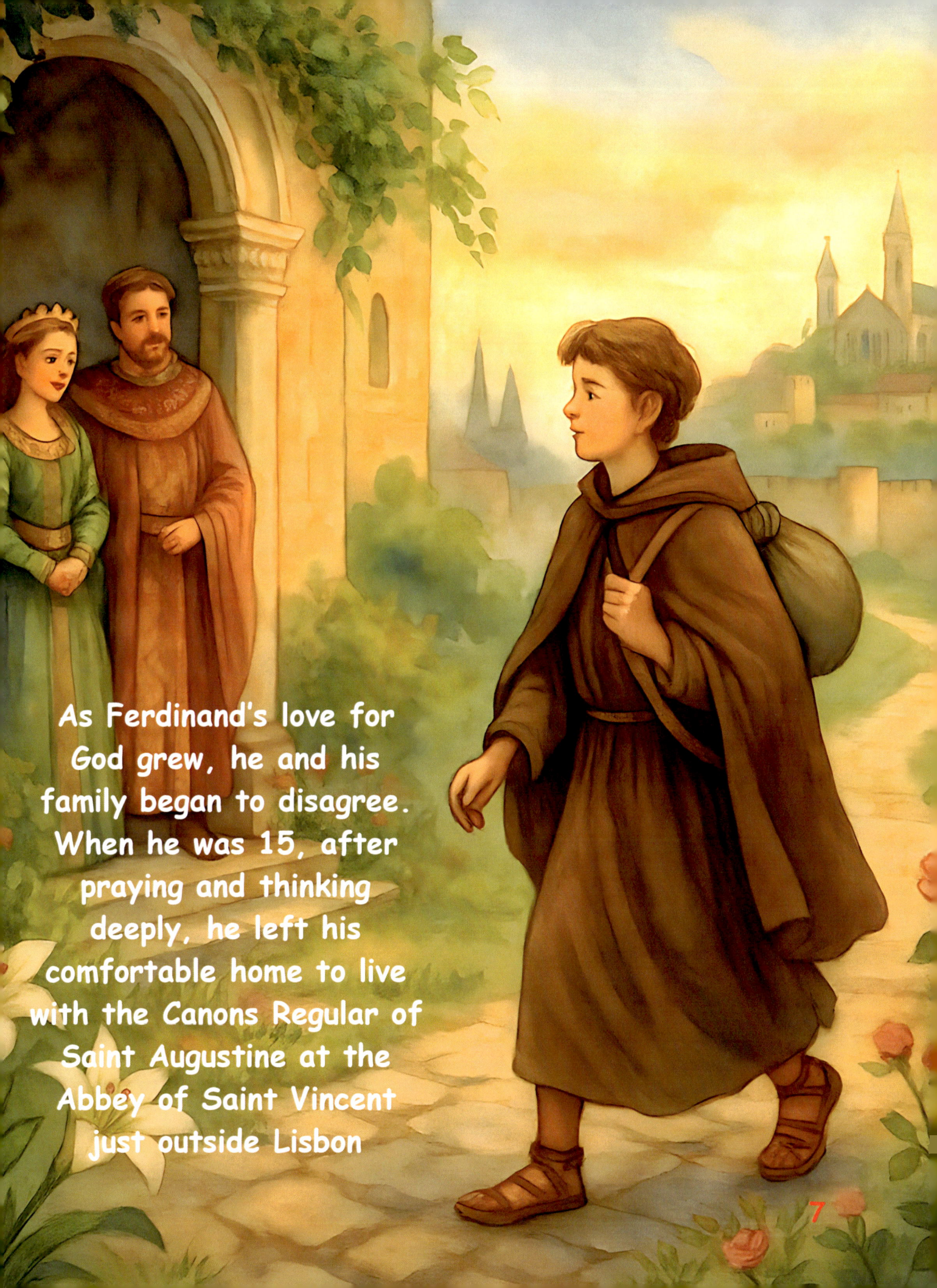

As Ferdinand's love for God grew, he and his family began to disagree. When he was 15, after praying and thinking deeply, he left his comfortable home to live with the Canons Regular of Saint Augustine at the Abbey of Saint Vincent just outside Lisbon

7

Monastic life brought little peace or focus for Ferdinand. The Abbey of St. Vincent was too close to home, so old friends and relatives visited often— bringing gifts that embarrassed him, dragging him into heated political discussions, and sharing distracting news of their social world. He could not find the quiet he needed, and his studies began to suffer

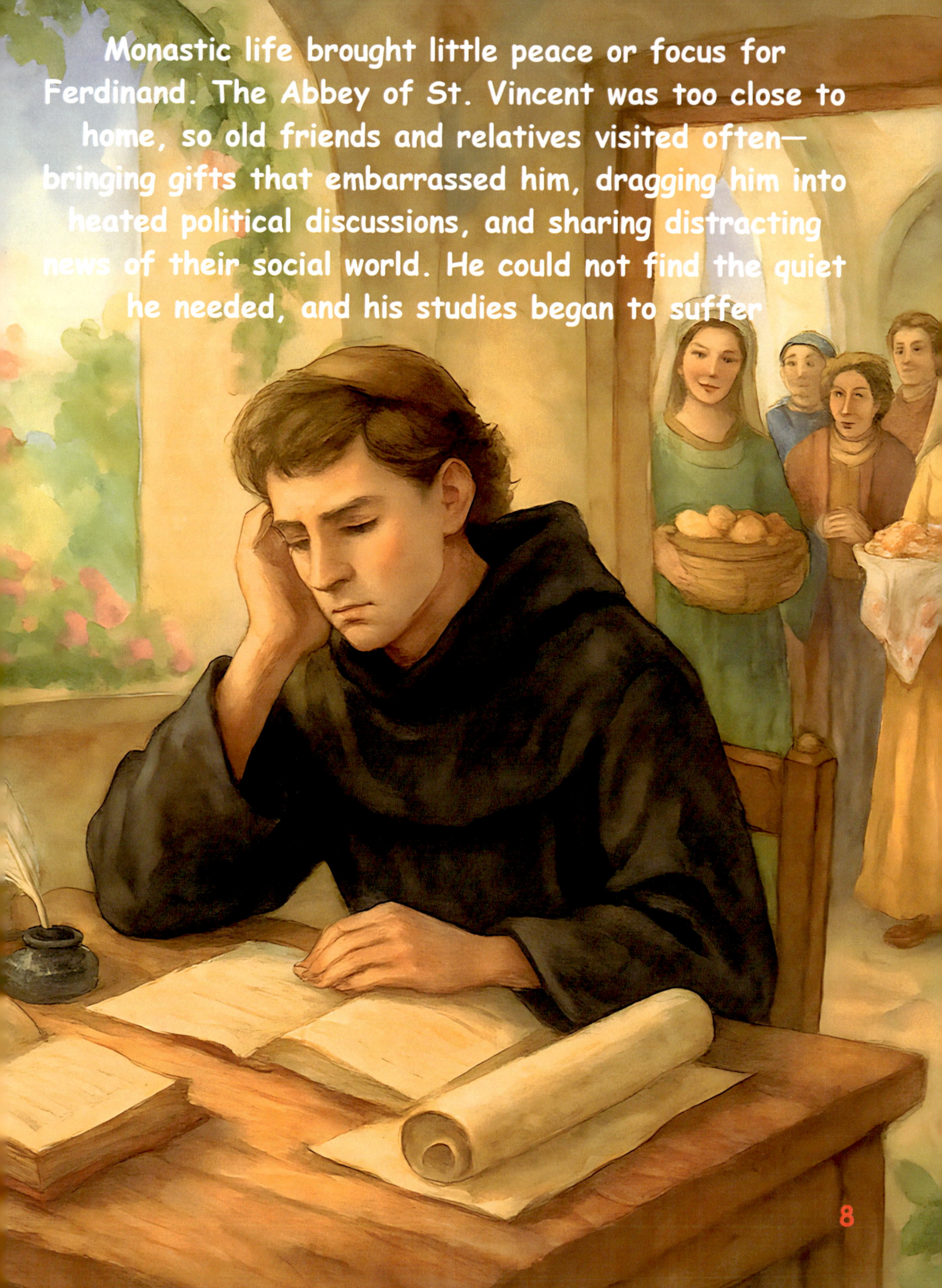

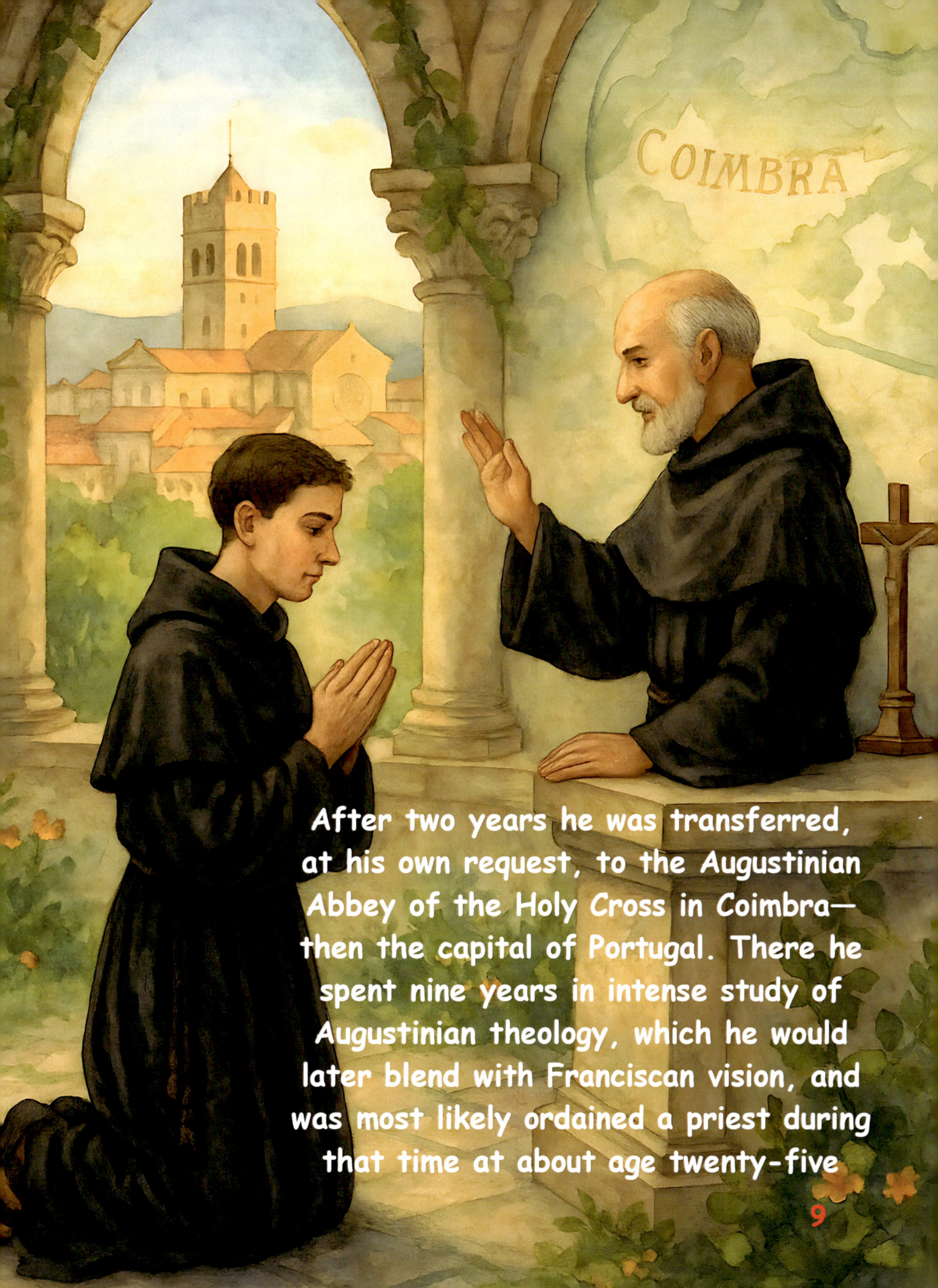

After two years he was transferred, at his own request, to the Augustinian Abbey of the Holy Cross in Coimbra— then the capital of Portugal. There he spent nine years in intense study of Augustinian theology, which he would later blend with Franciscan vision, and was most likely ordained a priest during that time at about age twenty-five

After he became a priest, Ferdinand helped take care of guests at the abbey. That's how he met the Franciscan friars. In 1219, he saw five of Saint Francis's friends who were going to Morocco to tell others about Jesus. Ferdinand was very impressed by how much they loved the Gospel and how simply they lived

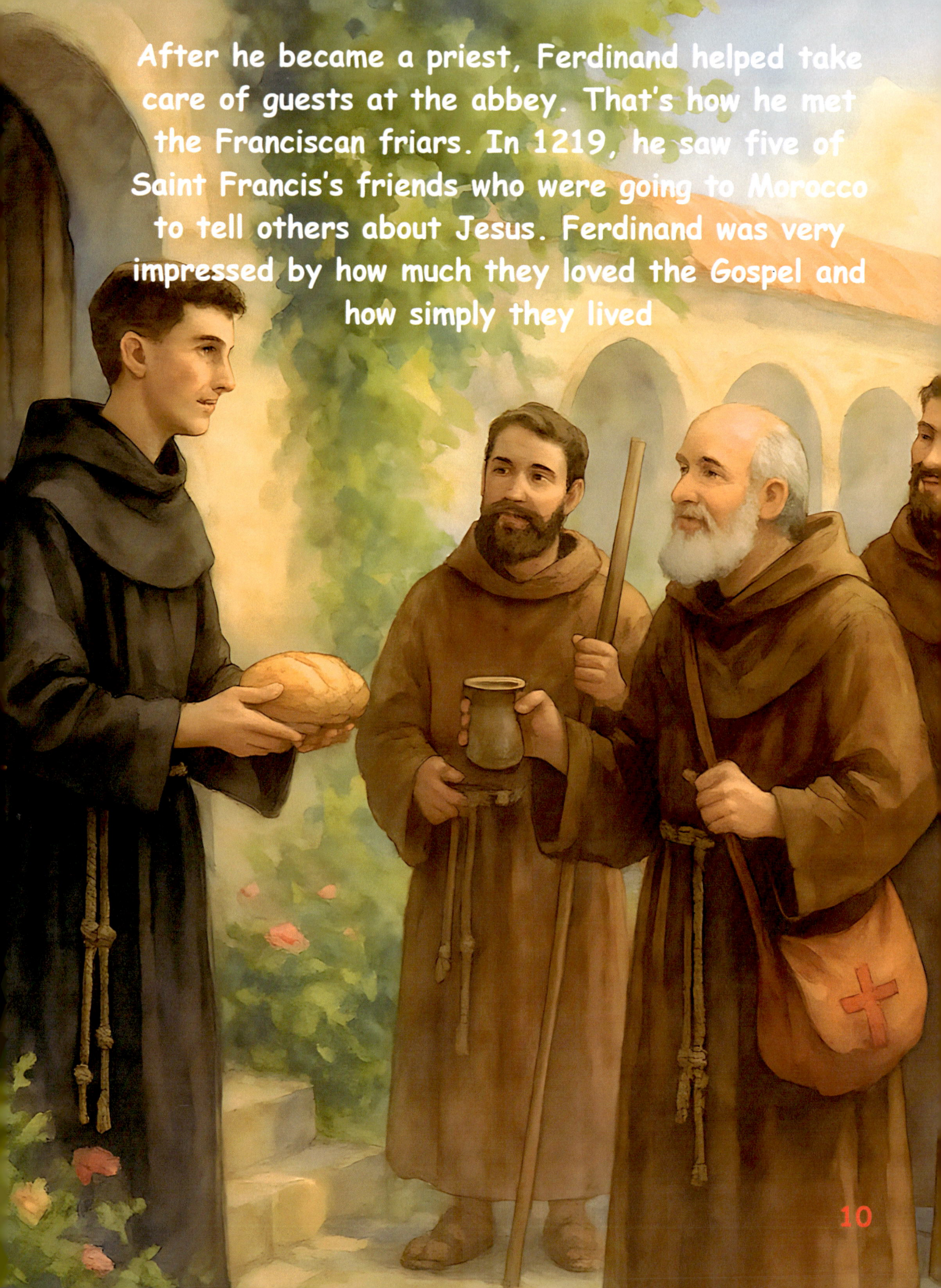

10

On February 1220, Ferdinand learned that five Franciscan friars he admired had been martyred in Morocco after boldly preaching Christ. Their bodies were returned to Portugal and enshrined in the Church of the Holy Cross in Coimbra. Deeply moved by their witness, he resolved to leave everything and follow Christ

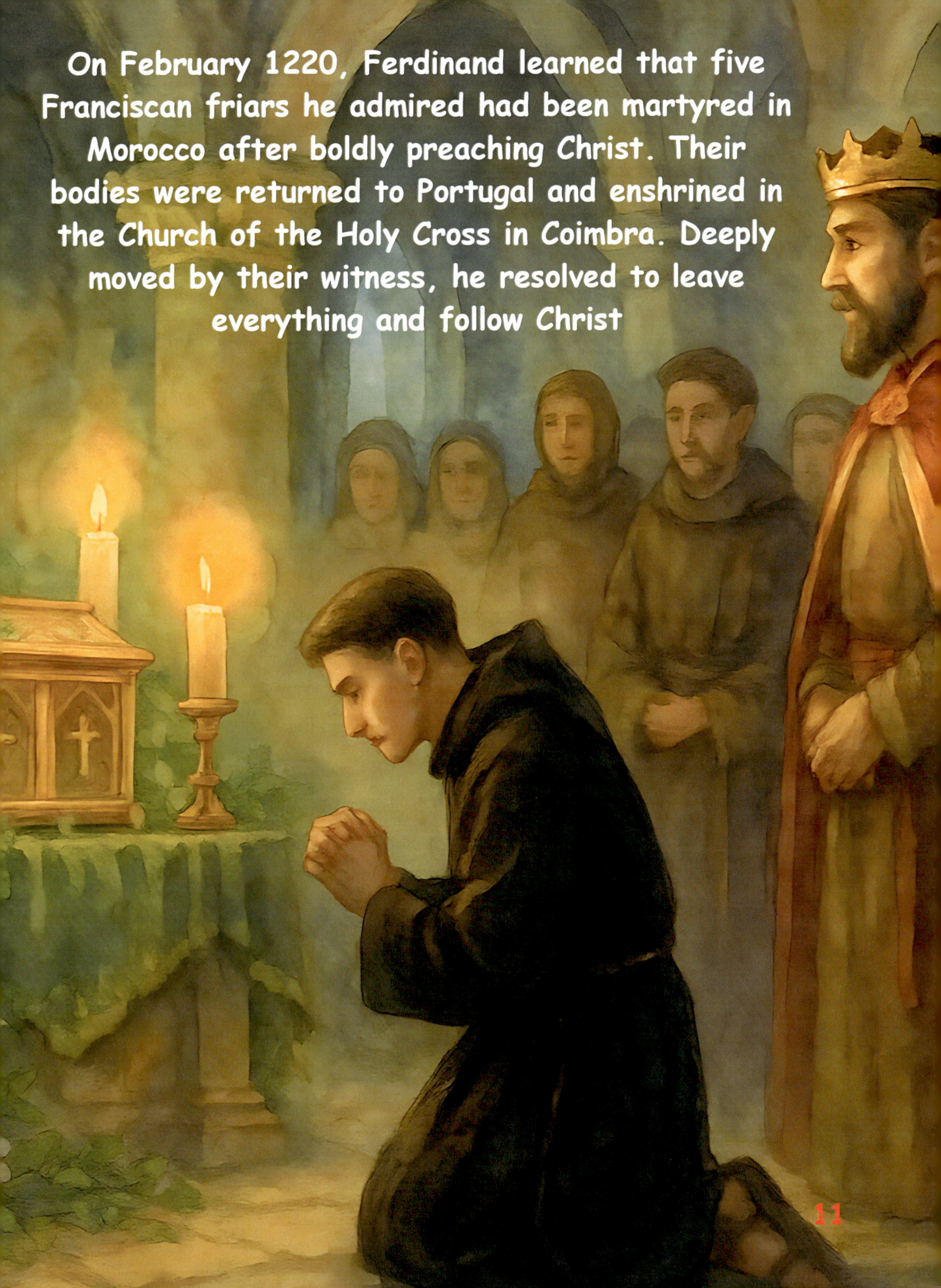

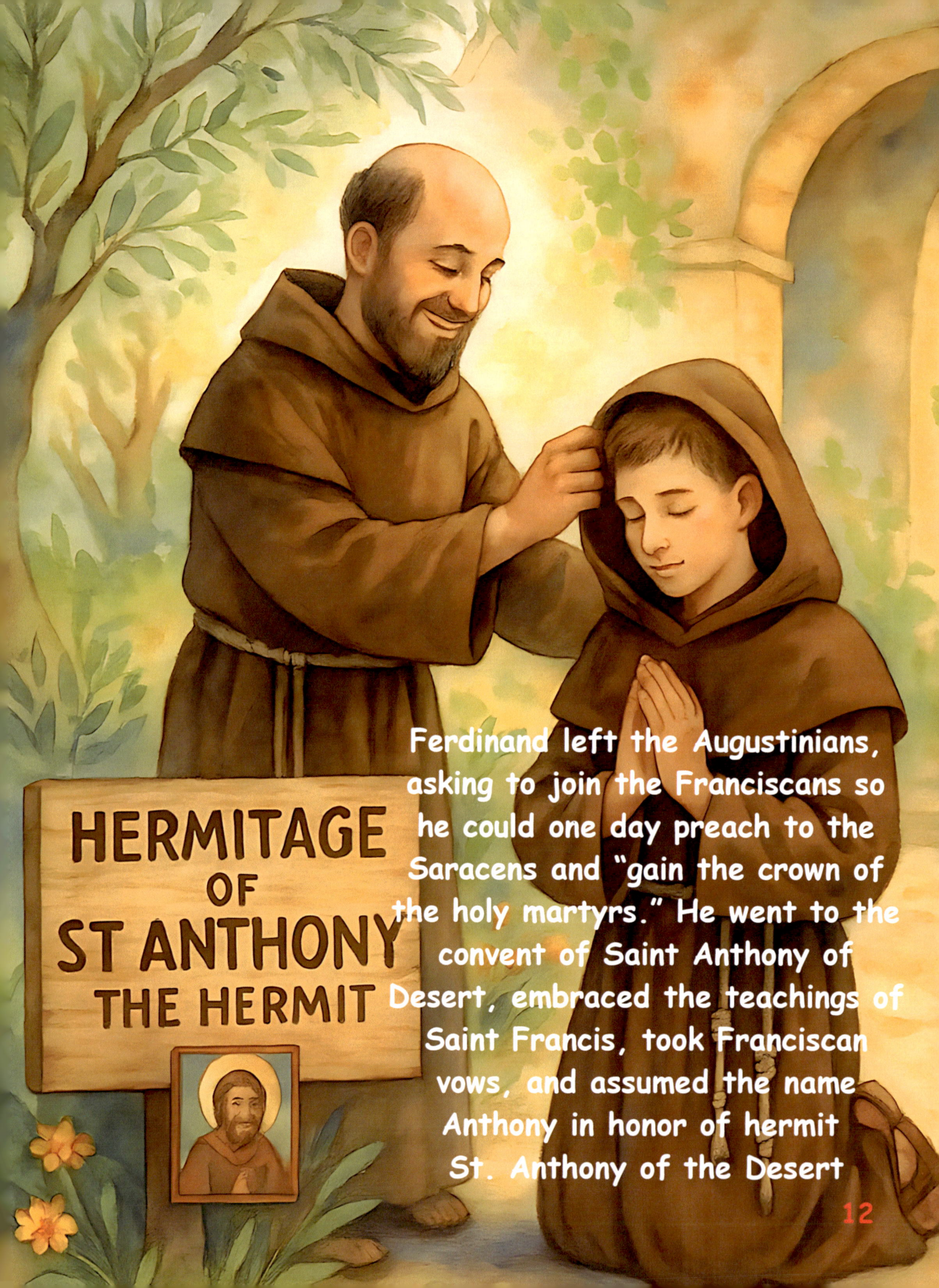

HERMITAGE
OF
ST ANTHONY
THE HERMIT

Ferdinand left the Augustinians, asking to join the Franciscans so he could one day preach to the Saracens and "gain the crown of the holy martyrs." He went to the convent of Saint Anthony of Desert, embraced the teachings of Saint Francis, took Franciscan vows, and assumed the name Anthony in honor of hermit St. Anthony of the Desert

12

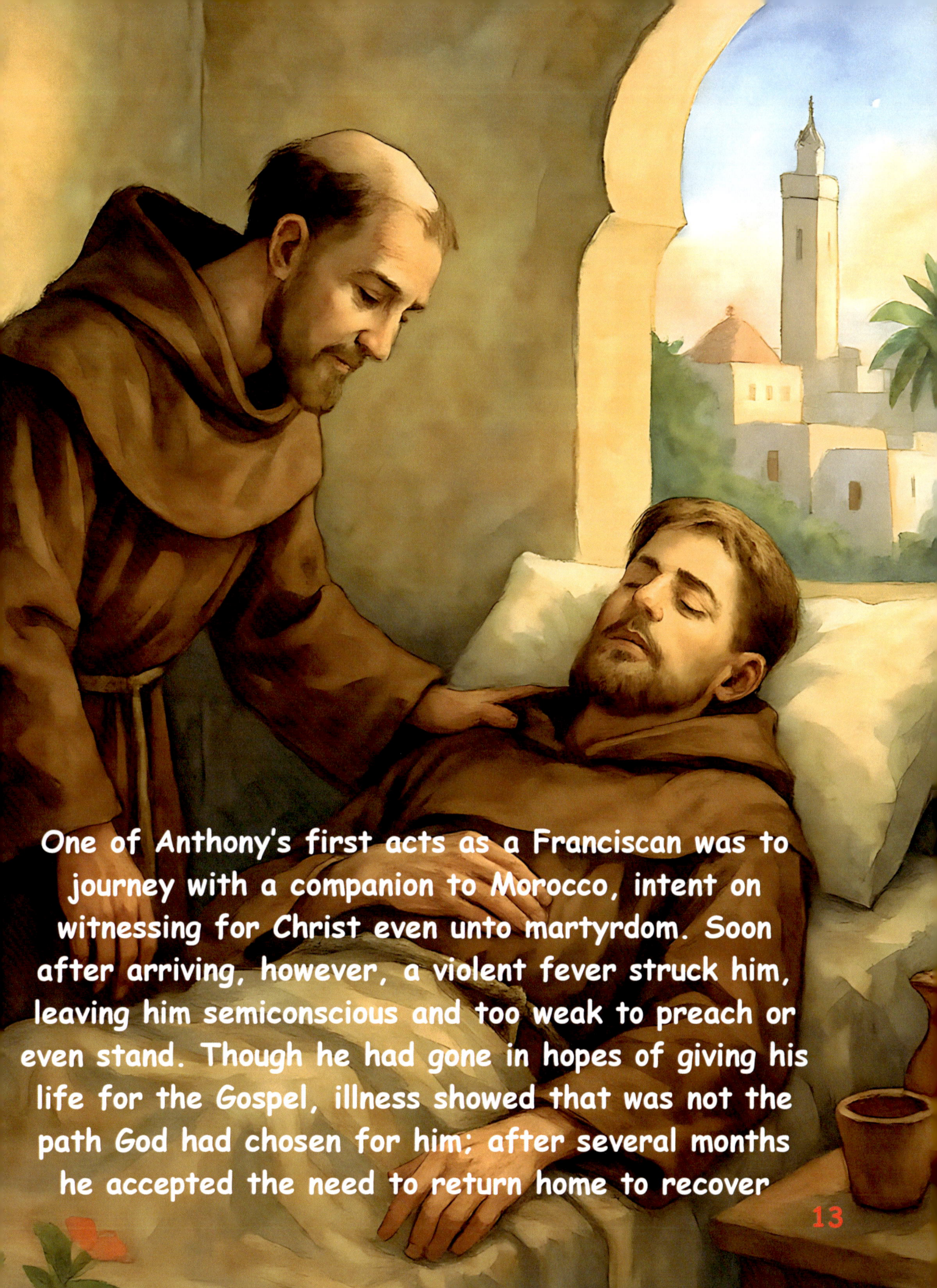

One of Anthony's first acts as a Franciscan was to journey with a companion to Morocco, intent on witnessing for Christ even unto martyrdom. Soon after arriving, however, a violent fever struck him, leaving him semiconscious and too weak to preach or even stand. Though he had gone in hopes of giving his life for the Gospel, illness showed that was not the path God had chosen for him; after several months he accepted the need to return home to recover

13

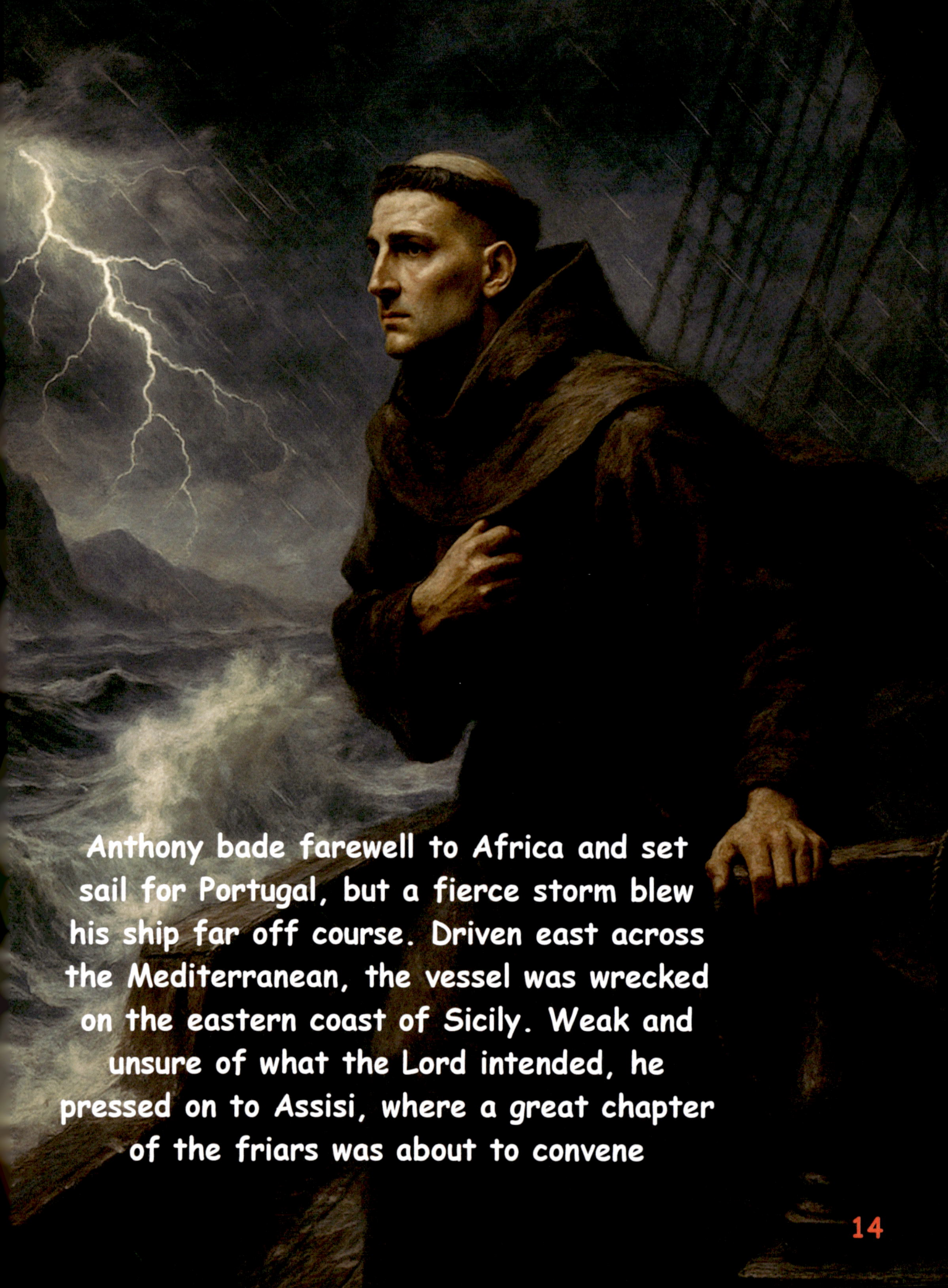

Anthony bade farewell to Africa and set sail for Portugal, but a fierce storm blew his ship far off course. Driven east across the Mediterranean, the vessel was wrecked on the eastern coast of Sicily. Weak and unsure of what the Lord intended, he pressed on to Assisi, where a great chapter of the friars was about to convene

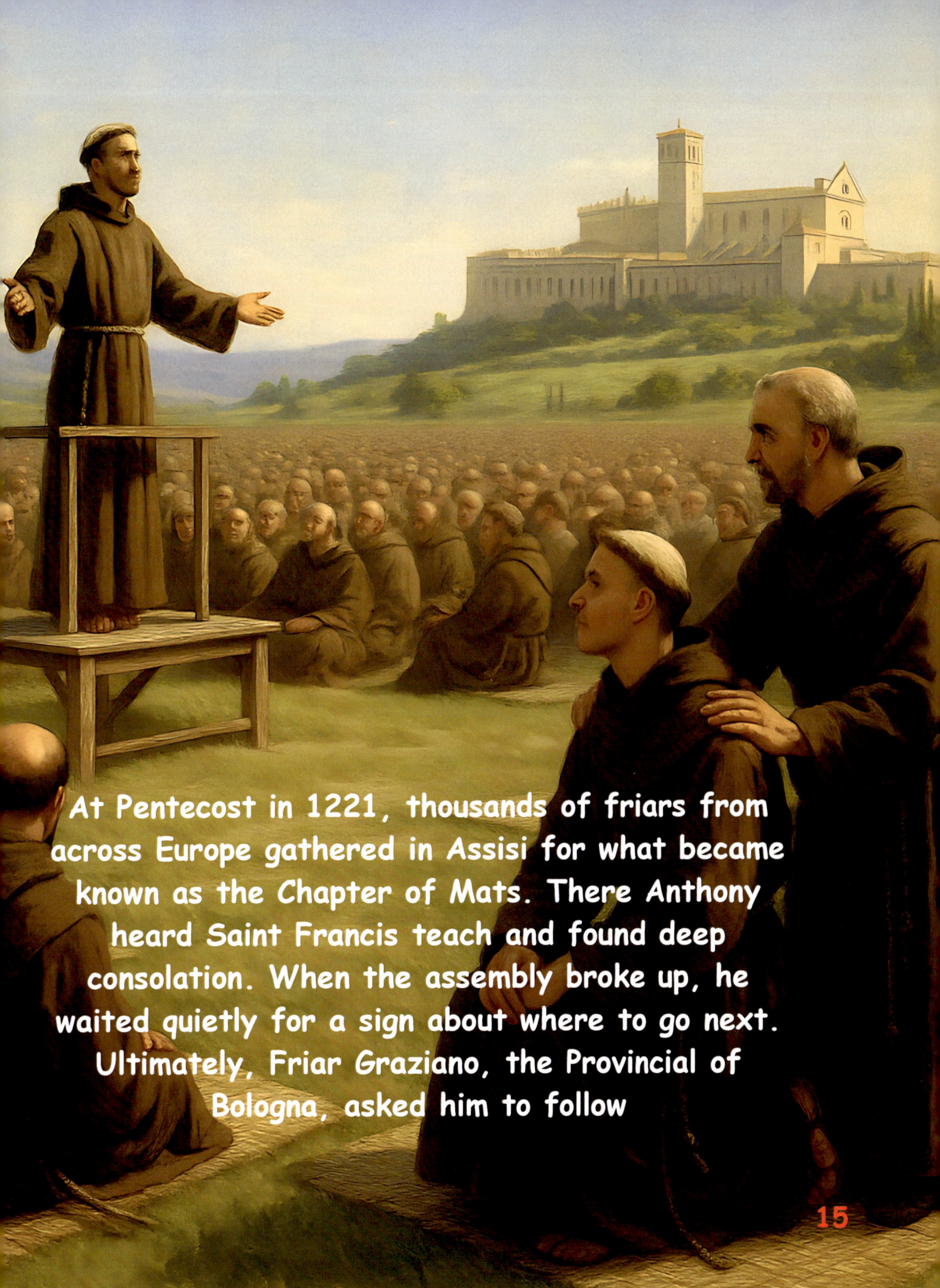

At Pentecost in 1221, thousands of friars from across Europe gathered in Assisi for what became known as the Chapter of Mats. There Anthony heard Saint Francis teach and found deep consolation. When the assembly broke up, he waited quietly for a sign about where to go next. Ultimately, Friar Graziano, the Provincial of Bologna, asked him to follow

Anthony went from Coimbra to Morocco, then Sicily, then Assisi, and ended up at a quiet hermitage in Montepaolo. There he found the calm he had been looking for and spent his days helping others and doing simple jobs like cooking and cleaning

In 1222, at a gathering for the ordination of Dominicans and Franciscans in the city of Forb, the scheduled preacher failed to appear. Friar Graziano, his provincial, asked the then-27-year-old Anthony—who was presumed uneducated—to give "just something simple." Though reluctant at first, Anthony spoke plainly, and soon the fire within him was unmistakable. His deep knowledge and, even more, the passionate intensity of his preaching astonished everyone. That moment marked the end of his quiet hermit life and the beginning of his public ministry

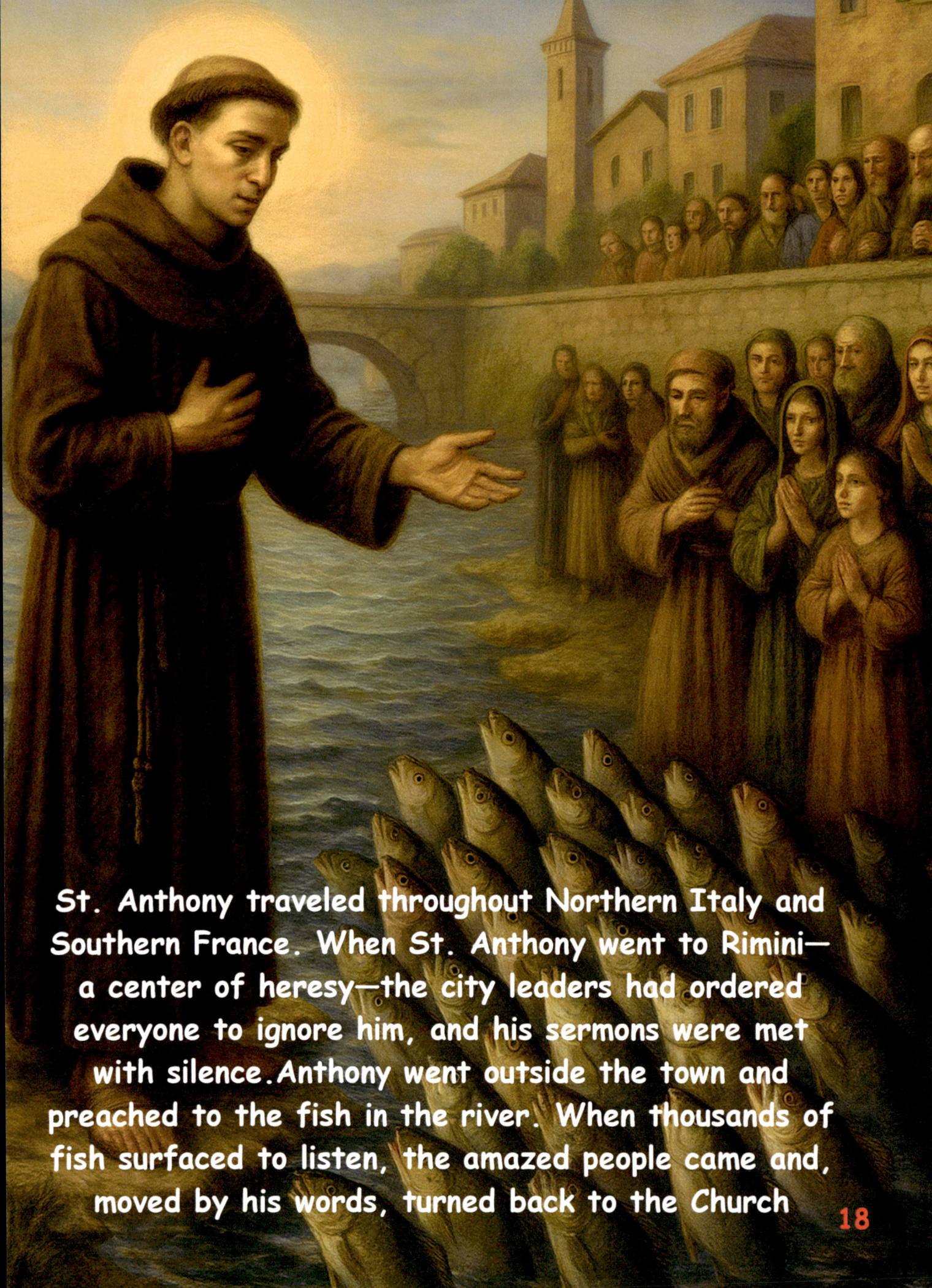

St. Anthony traveled throughout Northern Italy and Southern France. When St. Anthony went to Rimini—a center of heresy—the city leaders had ordered everyone to ignore him, and his sermons were met with silence. Anthony went outside the town and preached to the fish in the river. When thousands of fish surfaced to listen, the amazed people came and, moved by his words, turned back to the Church

18

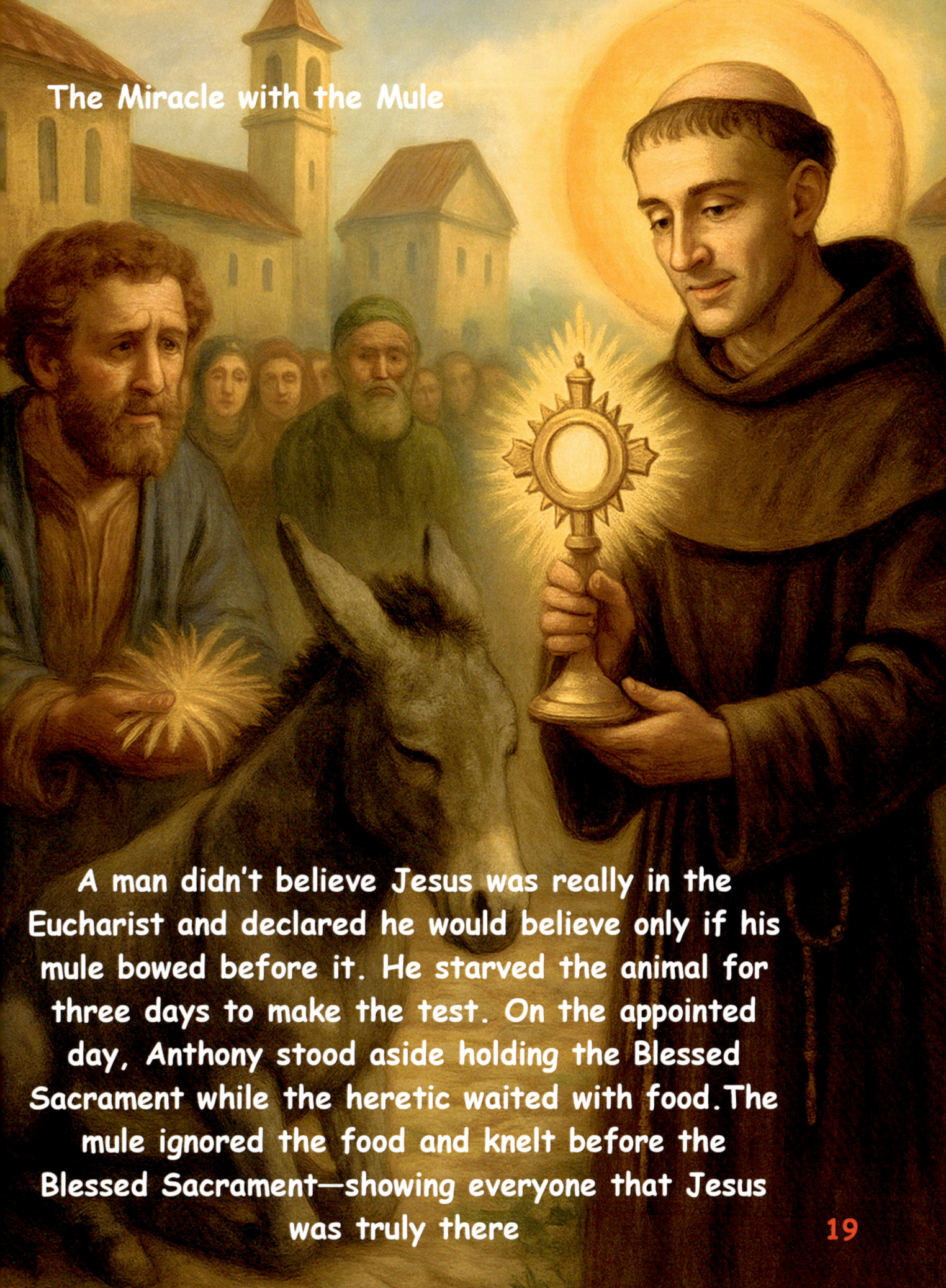

The Miracle with the Mule

A man didn't believe Jesus was really in the Eucharist and declared he would believe only if his mule bowed before it. He starved the animal for three days to make the test. On the appointed day, Anthony stood aside holding the Blessed Sacrament while the heretic waited with food. The mule ignored the food and knelt before the Blessed Sacrament—showing everyone that Jesus was truly there

19

A boy told Saint Anthony he had hurt his mother. Anthony spoke very seriously about respecting parents, and the boy misunderstood and hurt his own foot. His mother ran to Anthony in tears. Anthony prayed, and by God's grace the boy was healed and his foot made whole again

Saint Anthony:
Teacher, Preacher, and Doctor of Church

1224 – Chosen to Teach:
Saint Francis gives Anthony special blessing to teach the friars.

Teaching & Preaching:
He trains others while porverfully preaching to crowds

1226 – Leadership & Prayer:
Named provincial of northern Italy, yet still retreats to pray in solitude

Easter 1228 – Rome:
Anthony speaks before Pope Gregory IX; the reaction felt like a new Pentecost

Doctor of the Church:
Because of his teaching and love for God, he became one of only 36 Doctors of the Church

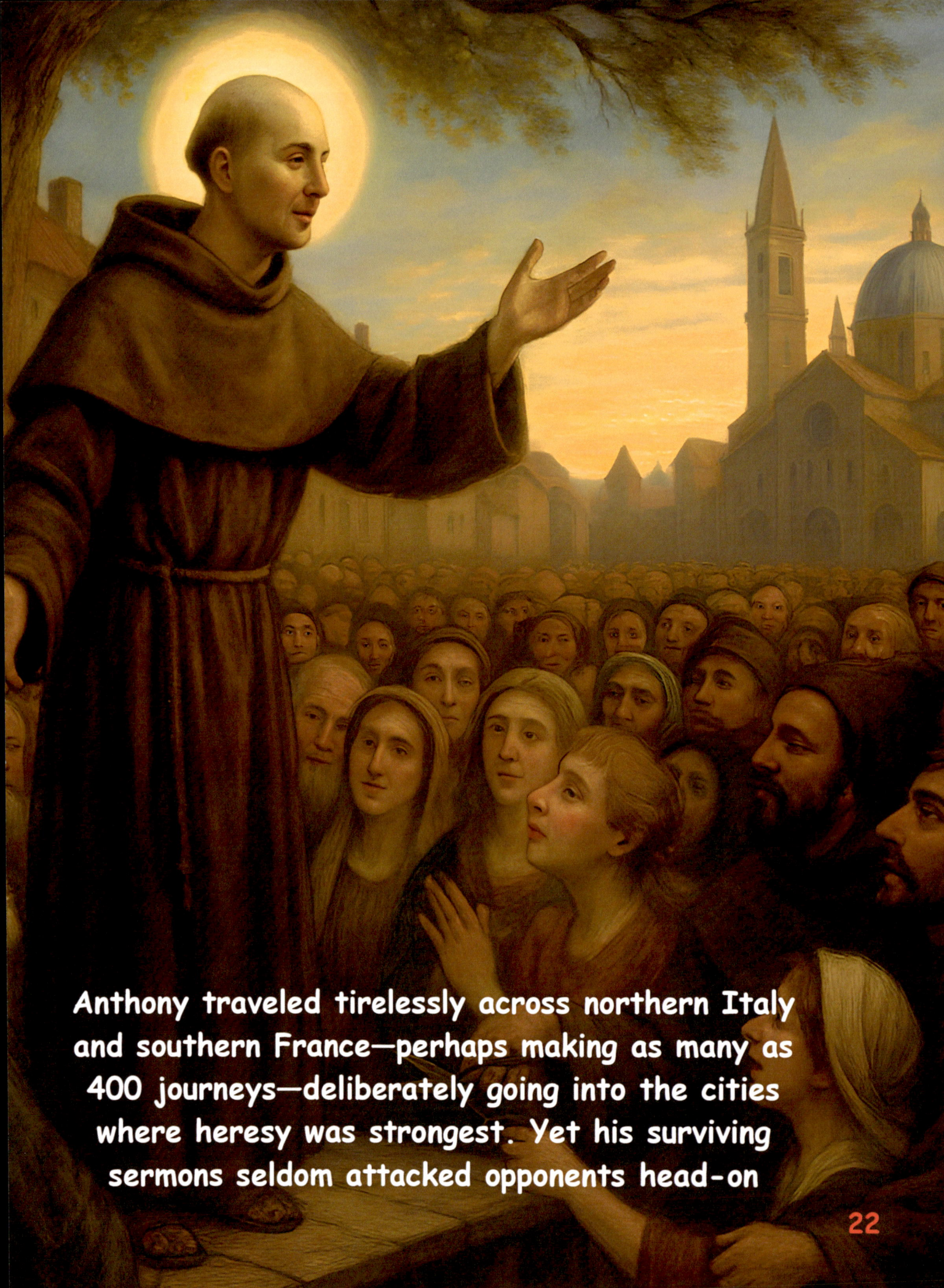

Anthony traveled tirelessly across northern Italy and southern France—perhaps making as many as 400 journeys—deliberately going into the cities where heresy was strongest. Yet his surviving sermons seldom attacked opponents head-on

In 1231, Saint Anthony returned to Padua and gave his last great Lent talks. So many people came—sometimes 30,000—that the churches couldn't hold them, so he spoke outside in the squares and fields. He had been sick many times and was very weak from dropsy, but he kept preaching and hearing people's confessions. During that season, he had a feeling that he wouldn't be with them much longer

23

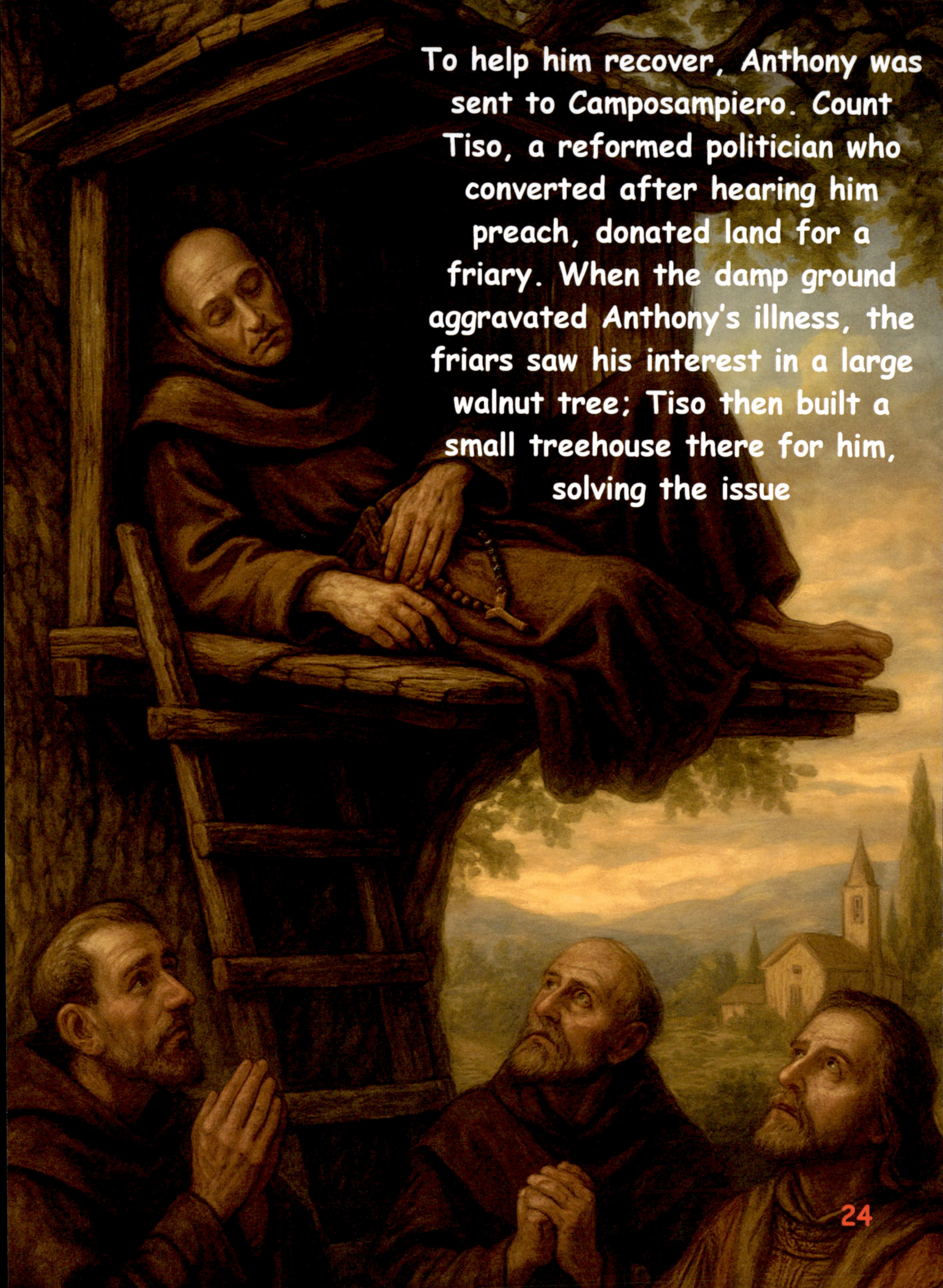

To help him recover, Anthony was sent to Camposampiero. Count Tiso, a reformed politician who converted after hearing him preach, donated land for a friary. When the damp ground aggravated Anthony's illness, the friars saw his interest in a large walnut tree; Tiso then built a small treehouse there for him, solving the issue

24

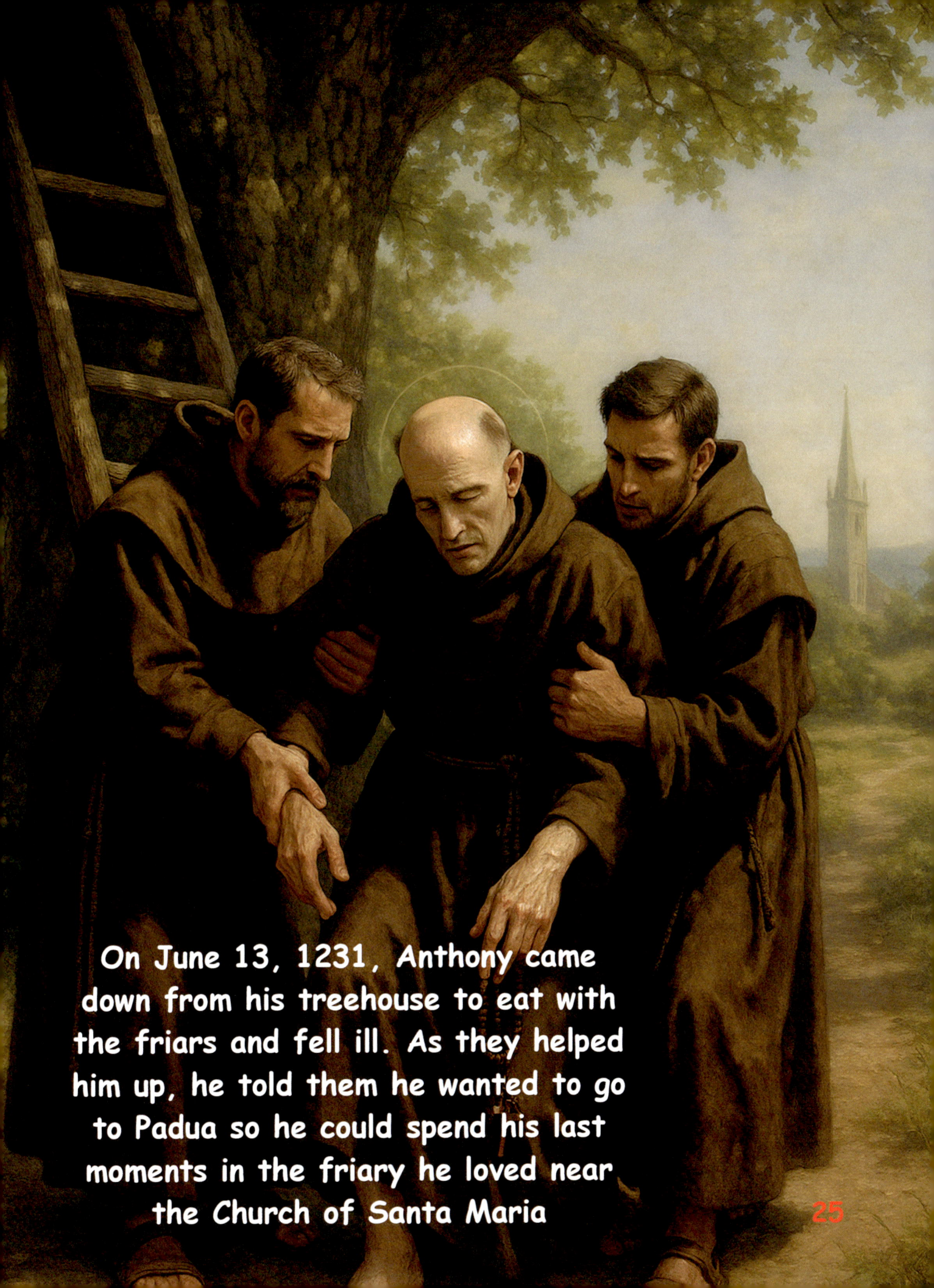

On June 13, 1231, Anthony came down from his treehouse to eat with the friars and fell ill. As they helped him up, he told them he wanted to go to Padua so he could spend his last moments in the friary he loved near the Church of Santa Maria

25

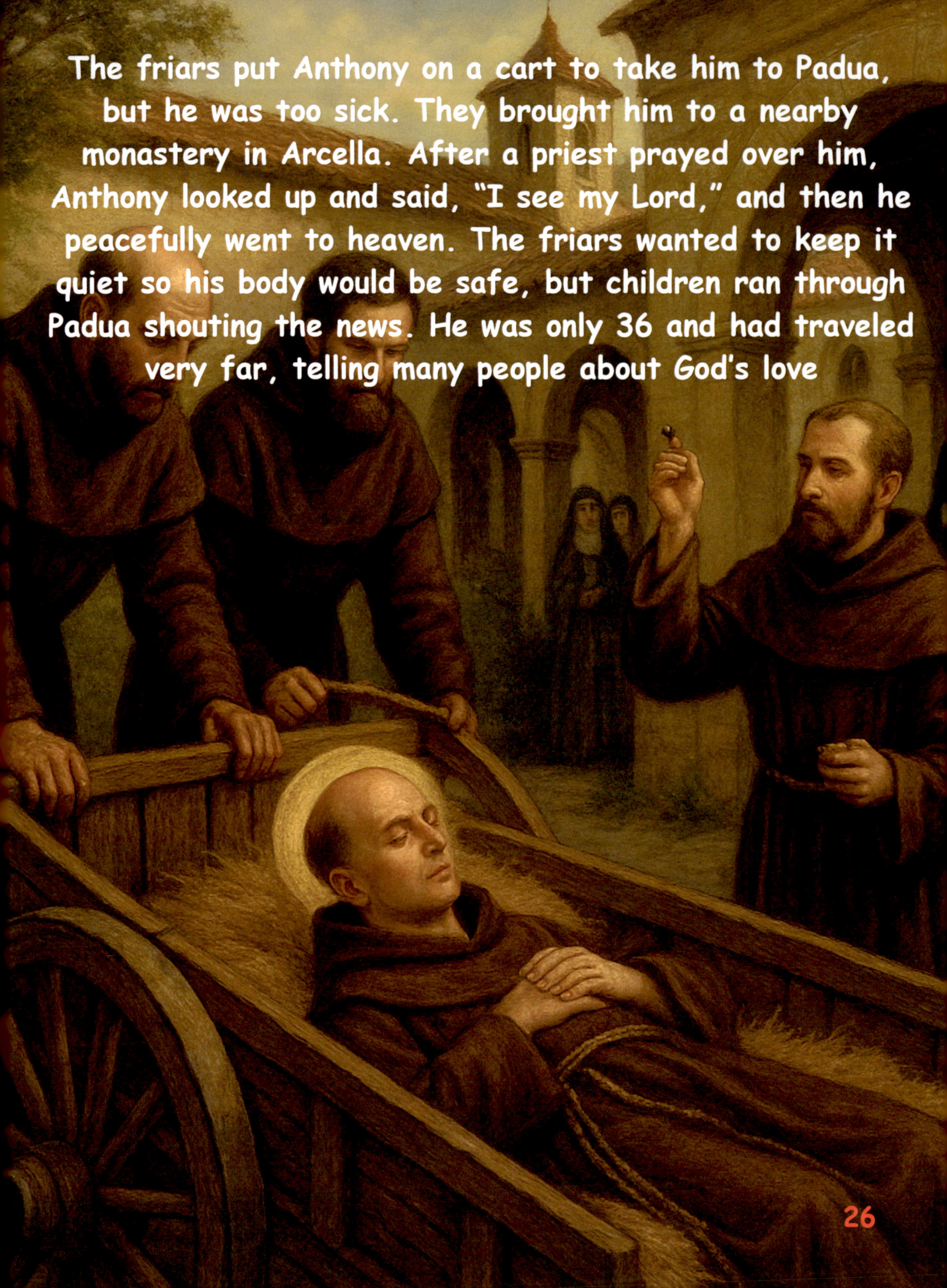

The friars put Anthony on a cart to take him to Padua, but he was too sick. They brought him to a nearby monastery in Arcella. After a priest prayed over him, Anthony looked up and said, "I see my Lord," and then he peacefully went to heaven. The friars wanted to keep it quiet so his body would be safe, but children ran through Padua shouting the news. He was only 36 and had traveled very far, telling many people about God's love

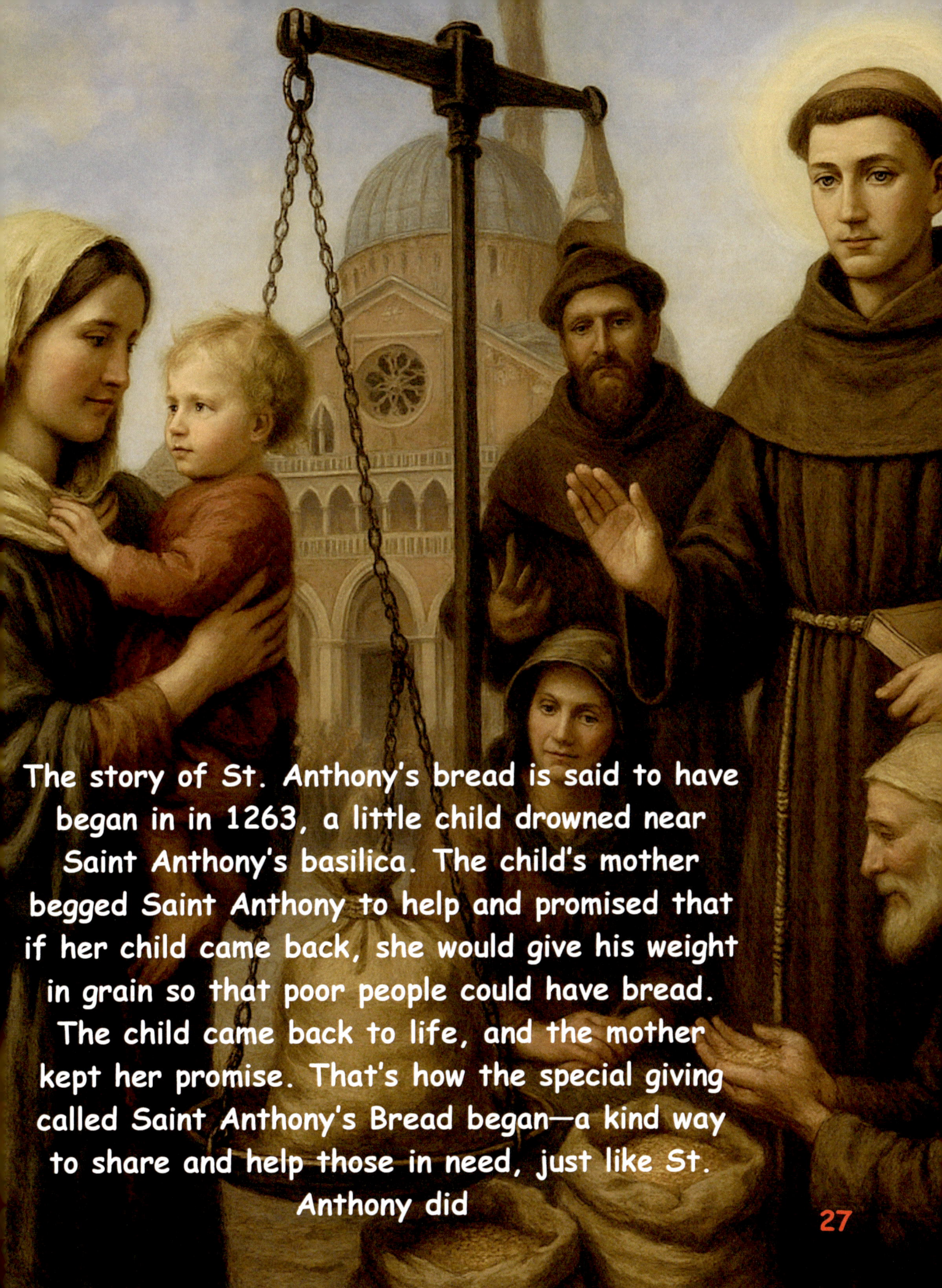

The story of St. Anthony's bread is said to have began in in 1263, a little child drowned near Saint Anthony's basilica. The child's mother begged Saint Anthony to help and promised that if her child came back, she would give his weight in grain so that poor people could have bread. The child came back to life, and the mother kept her promise. That's how the special giving called Saint Anthony's Bread began—a kind way to share and help those in need, just like St. Anthony did

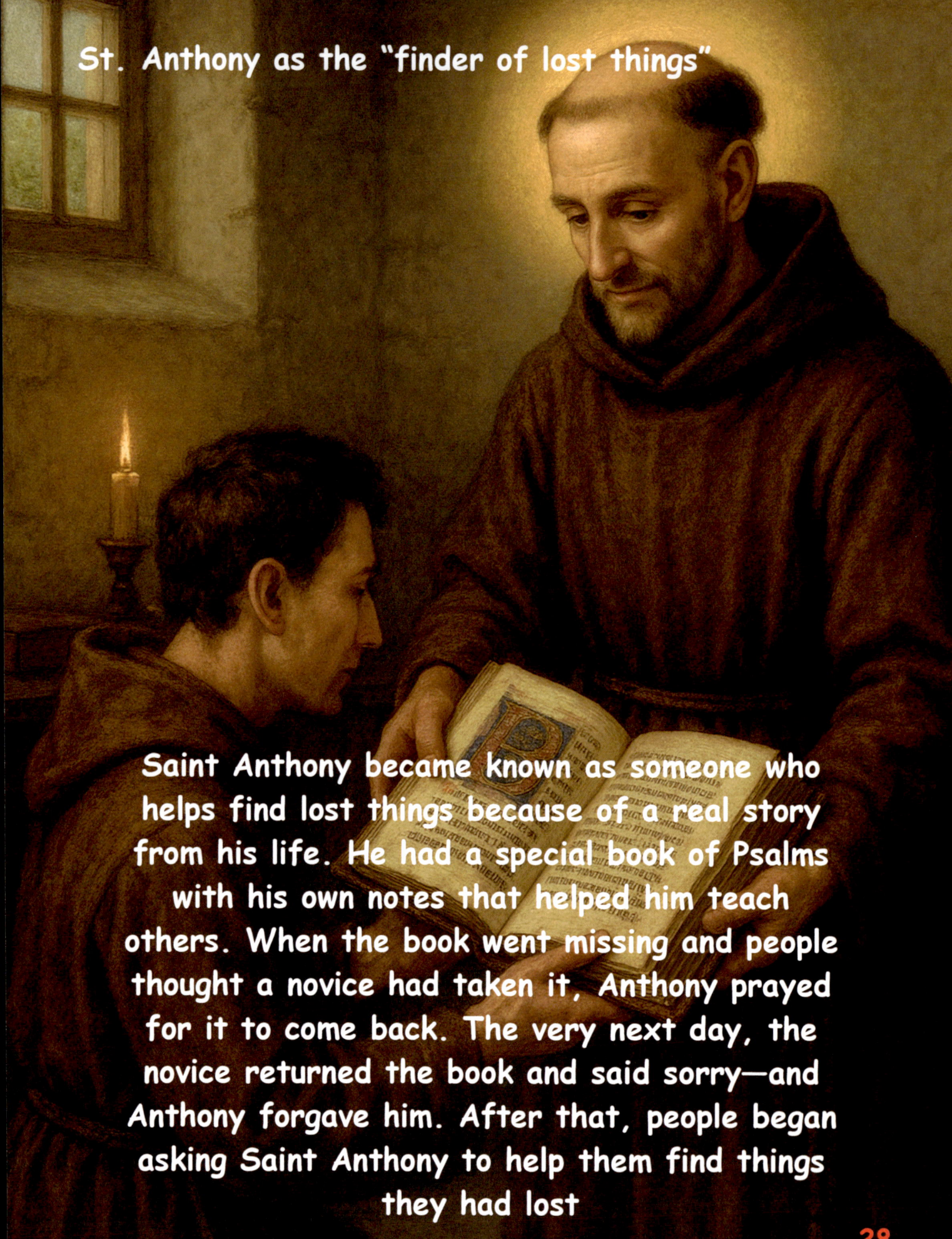

St. Anthony as the "finder of lost things"

Saint Anthony became known as someone who helps find lost things because of a real story from his life. He had a special book of Psalms with his own notes that helped him teach others. When the book went missing and people thought a novice had taken it, Anthony prayed for it to come back. The very next day, the novice returned the book and said sorry—and Anthony forgave him. After that, people began asking Saint Anthony to help them find things they had lost

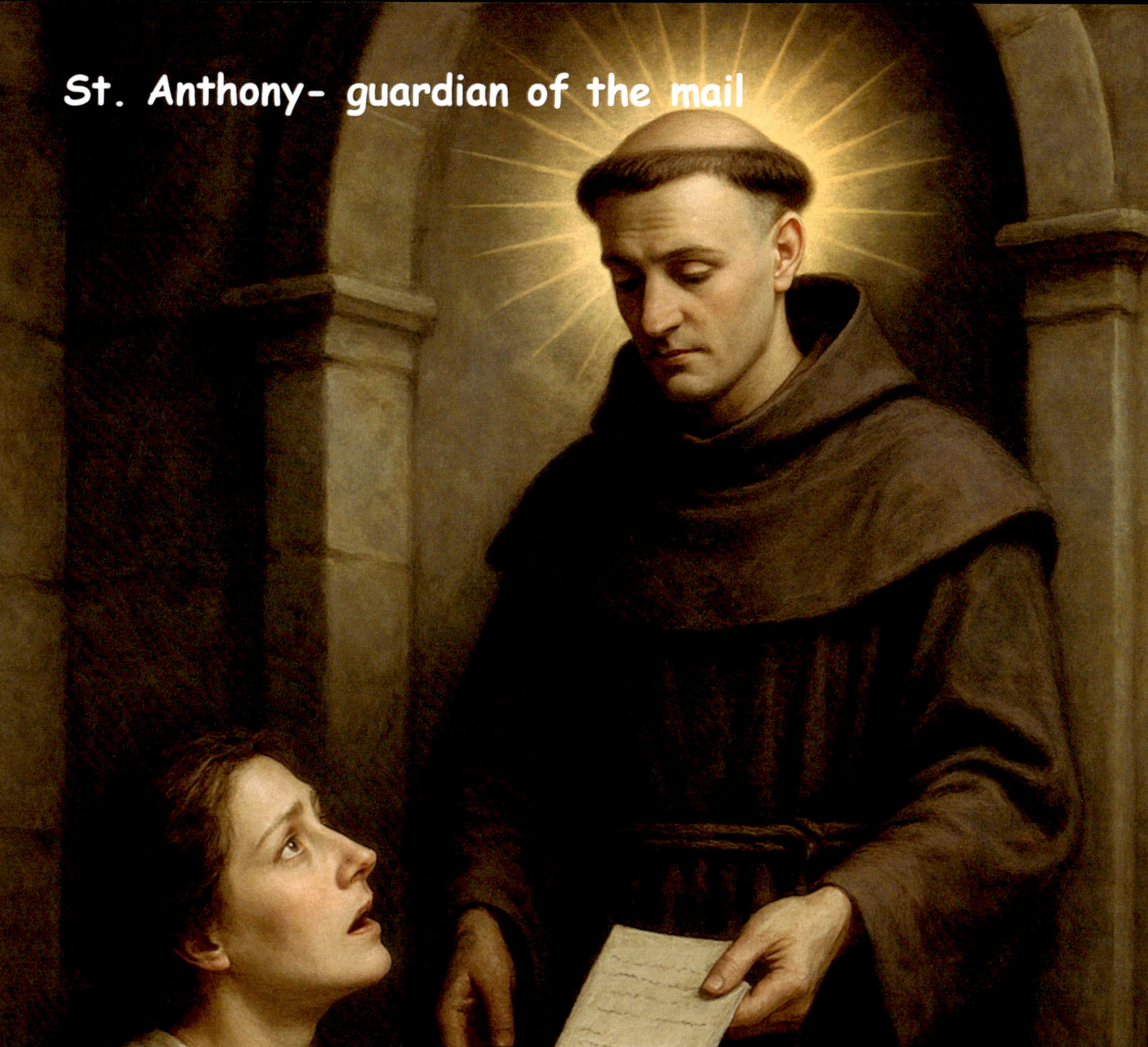

St. Anthony- guardian of the mail

Centuries later, in a legend from 1792, a heartbroken wife sought news of her husband, who had gone from Spain to Peru. After sending many letters with no reply, she prayed at the chapel of Saint Anthony, placing her latest letter in the hands of his statue and asking for his help. The next day she returned, disappointed to see her letter still there—until she lifted it and found it had been replaced by one from her husband. He wrote that a Franciscan priest had delivered her previous letter, and that he had feared she was dead. Her husband was overjoyed to hear from her

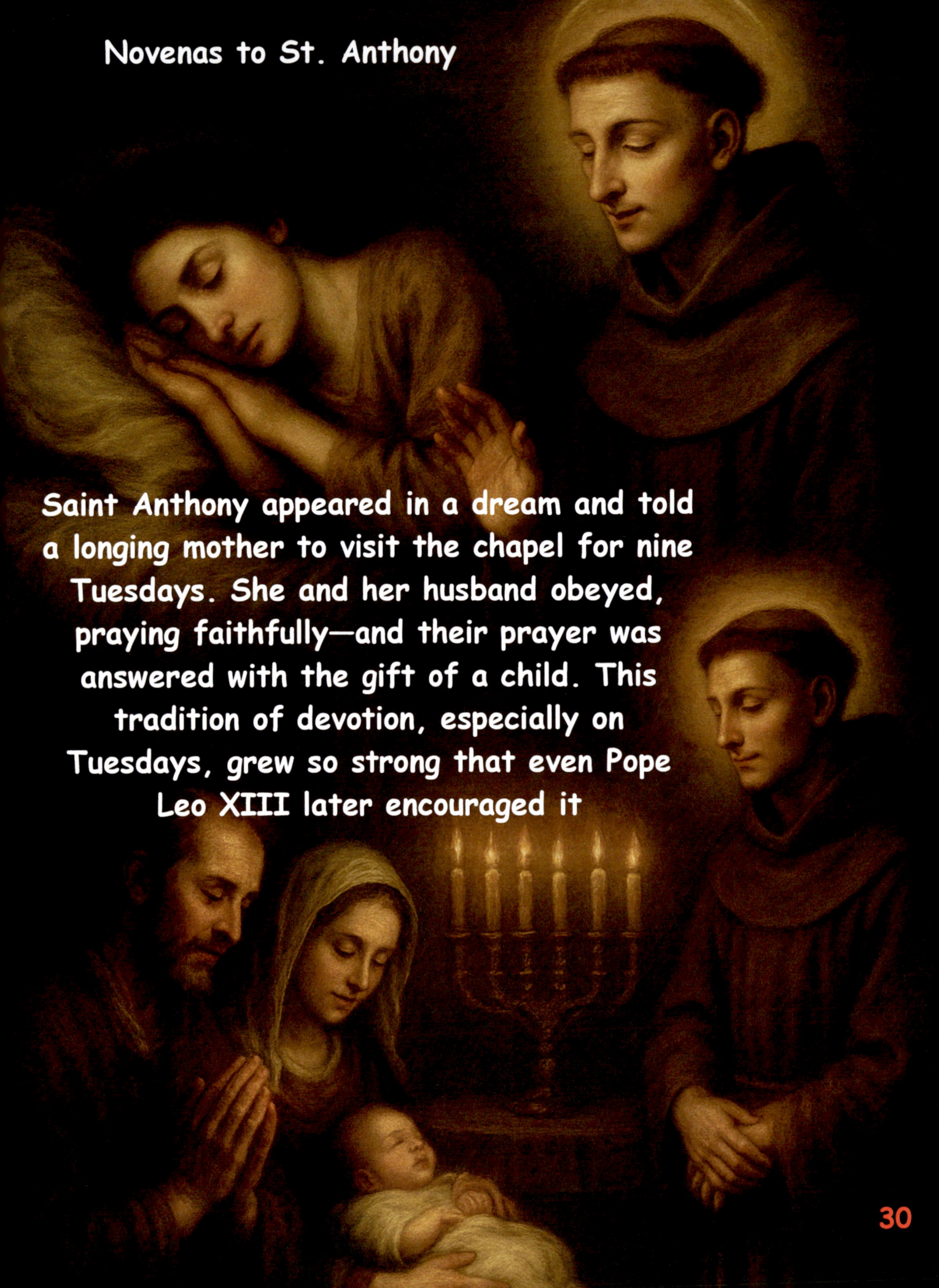

Saint Anthony appeared in a dream and told a longing mother to visit the chapel for nine Tuesdays. She and her husband obeyed, praying faithfully—and their prayer was answered with the gift of a child. This tradition of devotion, especially on Tuesdays, grew so strong that even Pope Leo XIII later encouraged it

St. Anthony and the Christ child

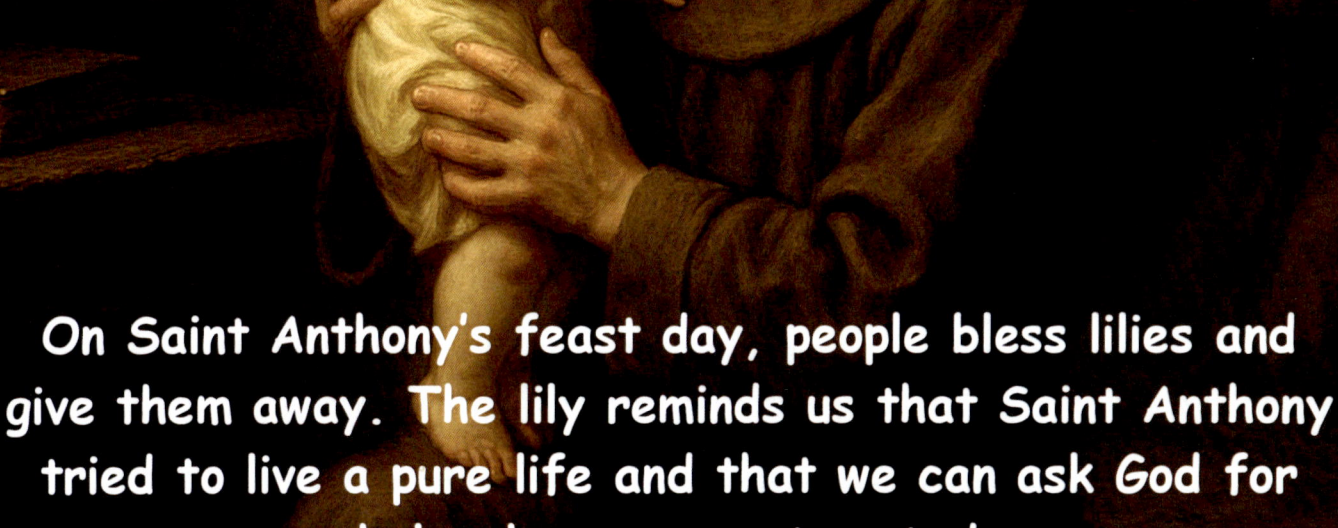

On Saint Anthony's feast day, people bless lilies and give them away. The lily reminds us that Saint Anthony tried to live a pure life and that we can ask God for help when we are tempted

One night, while Anthony was praying alone in a little hermitage, something amazing happened—Jesus appeared to him as a small child! The room lit up and filled with happy sounds. The owner of the place came to see what was happening and saw Anthony holding the child. When the vision ended, Anthony saw the man kneeling and quietly asked him not to tell anyone until after he had gone to heaven

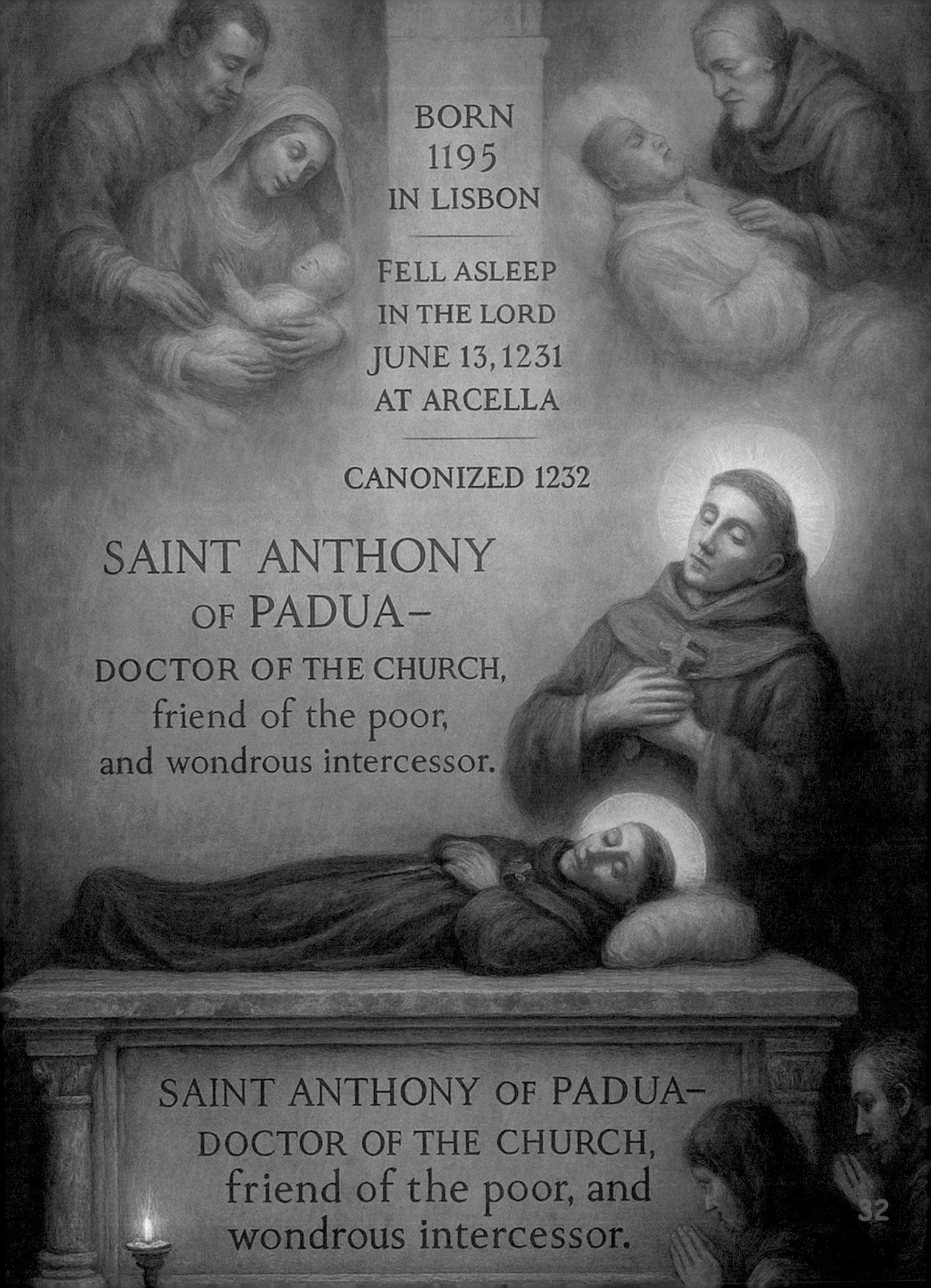

BORN
1195
IN LISBON

FELL ASLEEP
IN THE LORD
JUNE 13, 1231
AT ARCELLA

CANONIZED 1232

SAINT ANTHONY
OF PADUA –
DOCTOR OF THE CHURCH,
friend of the poor,
and wondrous intercessor.

SAINT ANTHONY OF PADUA–
DOCTOR OF THE CHURCH,
friend of the poor, and
wondrous intercessor.

32

Novena to Saint Anthony,

Dear Saint Anthony, You loved Jesus and helped others with gentle care.

Please help me with (my request).

Thank you for listening, and help me grow closer to Jesus every day.

Amen.

(Our Father, Hail Mary, Glory Be)

SAINT STEP: Do one small act of kindness today.

SAINT ANTHONY ACTIVITY BOOK

Welcome, little artist! These fun activity pages help you learn about Saint Anthony while you play, color, and explore. Here's what each one is:

Color the Page

Use your favorite crayons, markers, or pencils to color the whole scene any way you like. There's no right or wrong—just have fun being creative!

Color by Number

Follow the number key to color Saint Anthony and his lilies. Each number matches a color (like 1 = yellow, 2 = white) so the picture comes to life just right!

Spot the Difference

Look carefully at the two pictures. Can you find the small changes between them? Circle or color the differences you spot.

Maze

Help Saint Anthony's friend (or a letter, novice, etc.) find their way through the path. Start at the beginning and trace the correct route to the end.

Find the Hidden

Search the picture to find hidden items (like lilies or symbols of Saint Anthony). They might be tucked behind bushes, in windows, or hiding in plain sight!

35

37

39

41

42

HELP SAINT ANTHONY GET TO THE CHAPEL

START

END

SPOT THE DIFFERENCE

Find the Hidden Lilies

(lily image)	Lily
(book image)	Book
	Bread
(bread image)	Fish

Match the Saint Anthony Symbols

Help the novice return the Psalter to Saint Anthony

PSALTER

SPOT THE DIFFERENCE

CONNECT THE DOTS

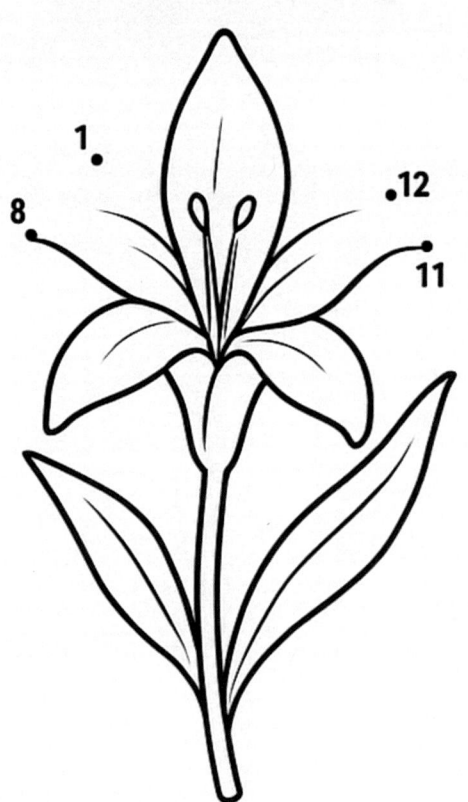

1.
.12
8.
11

MATCHING GAME

—— LILY

—— BOOK

—— BREAD

—— FISH

SPOT THE DIFFERENCE:
THE FOOT MIRACLE

 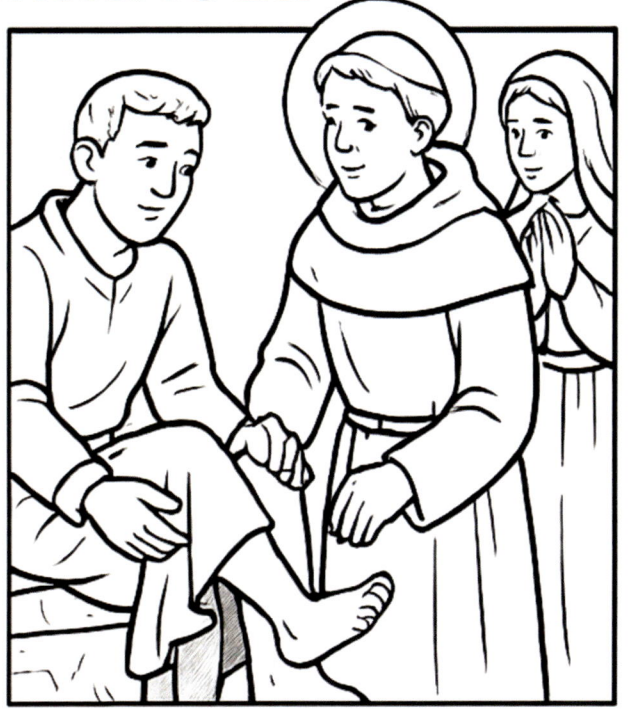

FIND SAINT ANTHONY'S SYMBOLS

HELP THE LETTER REACH PERU

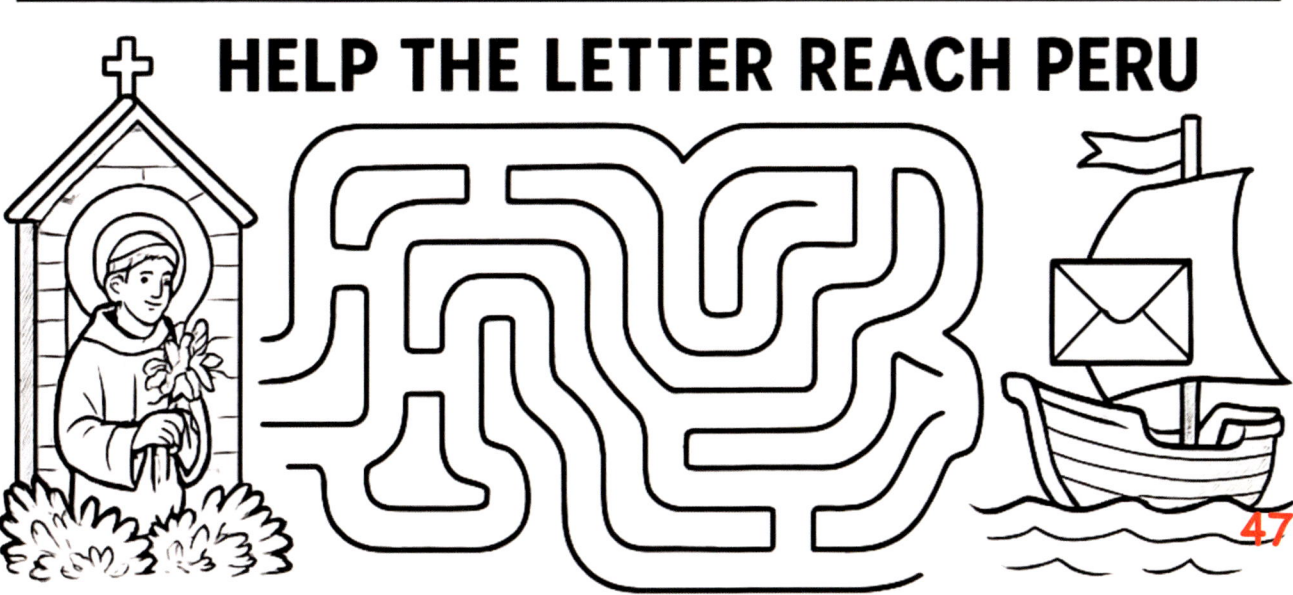

Spot the Difference

Color by Number

Color Saint Anthony and Lilies

1 yellow
2 white
3 brown
4 light blue
5 peach

48

SPOT THE DIFFERENCE
THE VISION OF JESUS

COLOR BY NUMBER:
SAINT ANTHONY AND LILIES

1	1 yellow
2	2 white
3	3 brown
4	4 light blue
5	5 peach

49

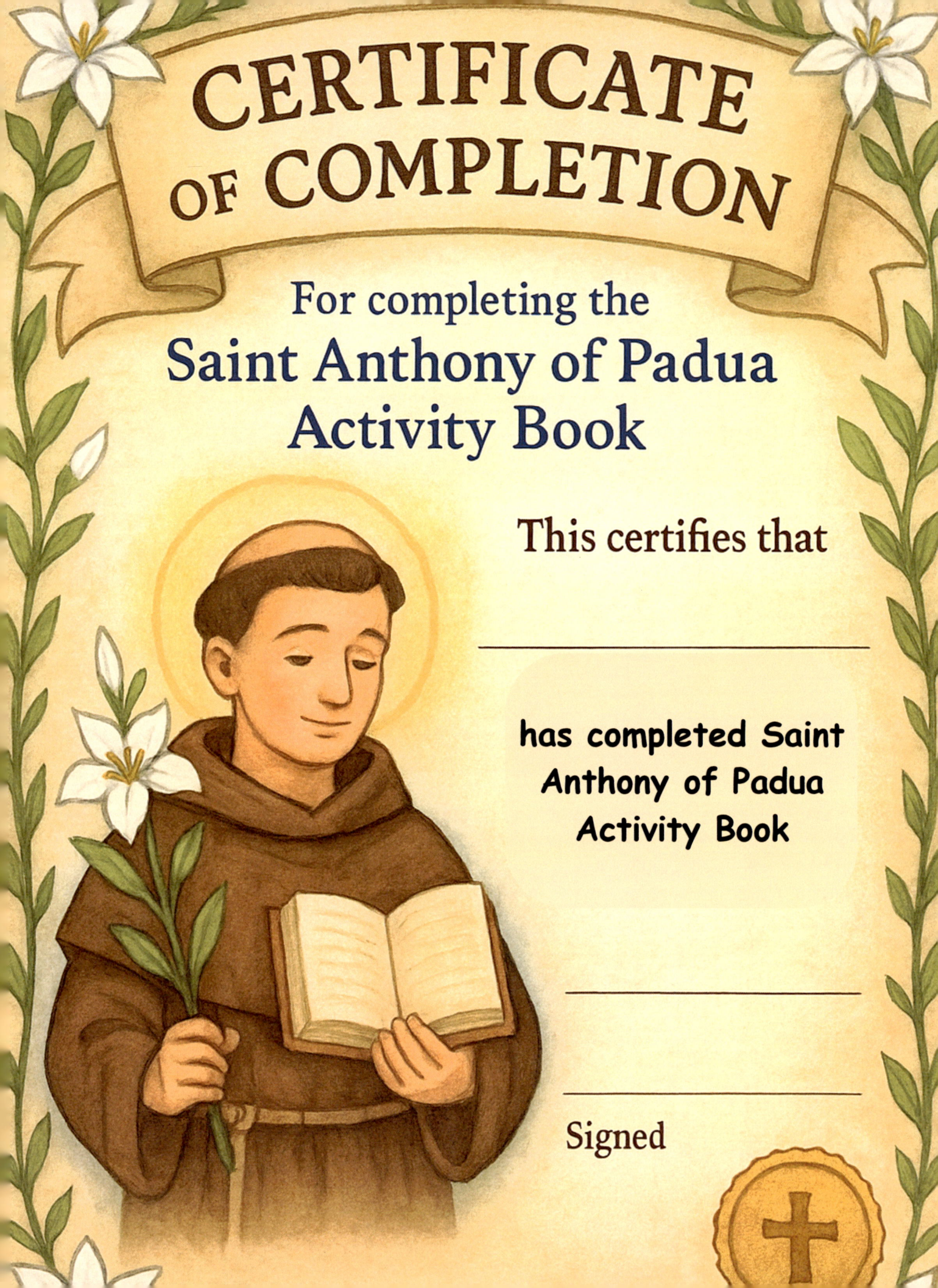

CERTIFICATE
OF COMPLETION

For completing the
Saint Anthony of Padua Activity Book

This certifies that

_____

has completed Saint
Anthony of Padua
Activity Book

_____

_____

Signed

Dr. Diya Abraham, Ph.D

A researcher at heart and mentor by calling, Dr. Diya Abraham earned her doctorate in Neuroscience from the Max Planck Institute in Germany and completed a post-doctoral fellowship at the University of California, San Francisco. Her work on circadian rhythms—the genes that keep our inner clocks in sync—has appeared in leading peer-reviewed journals and has been showcased on international conference stages

Dr. Abraham weaves science into faith-infused learning experiences. Through Bee Little Curious, the company she founded to enrich curious minds & soul, she creates evidence-based educational resources and uplifting religious products. She partners with parish schools to embed STEM principles into grace-filled curricula.

Joby James

Joby James has built an illustrious career at the intersection of engineering, enterprise-class cybersecurity sales and tech entrepreneurship. As the founder of cybersecurity firm, his team helps companies safeguard data while equipping organizations to navigate the digital world safely and responsibly

Joby believes that safeguarding souls matters just as much as protecting systems—a conviction nurtured through years of mentoring youth groups, where he first shared the saint stories that now inspire his writing.

Enquiries: info@beelittlecurious.com

www.ingramcontent.com/pod-product-compliance
Lightning Source LLC
Chambersburg PA
CBRC090828120626
46547CB00008B/626